La... of
COFFEE

Text by Frederick Hall • *Drawings by Peter Butterfield*

ENCYCLOPAEDIA BRITANNICA PRESS

CHICAGO   NEW YORK   LONDON

The true-to-life photographs in this book are from the educational motion picture "Brazil: People of the Highlands," produced by Encyclopaedia Britannica Films, Inc., and photographed in Brazil by Eric Pavel. The publishers are indebted to Mr. José Medeiros Pacheco, Brazilian Coffee Institute, New York, for supplying the photograph of a coffee "taster" on page 24 and for much valuable information, and also to Mr. José Viviani Telles, Vice Consul of Brazil, Chicago, for kindly reading the manuscript.

Frederick Hall, who wrote the text of this book, is an authority on Brazil. He went there for a visit of six months and stayed for nearly ten years! During his stay he lived for some time on a coffee plantation.

The design of this book is by Alex D'Amato. Supervision of color reproduction is by James Lockhart. The cover design is by Don Walkoe.

The book has been carefully manufactured for long wear. The paper is 100-pound coated stock specially created for this series. The pages are side-sewn and are fixed into the case with sturdy end sheets. The body type of the book is Caledonia.

Many families live and work on a Brazilian coffee plantation.

The coffee plantation of Santa Bárbara lies more than two hundred miles inland from the Atlantic coast of Brazil in South America. Here it is always warm by day, though often cold at night. The soil is rich and grows fine coffee.

The red earth is like powder, and when the wind blows, clouds of red dust fill the air. The dust seeps into pockets and shoes, and under hats.

Lúcia Ferreira lives with her family on the plantation, or *fazenda*. She is thirteen years old. When she was only eight, she started working in the fields with her father. He has to care for 8000 coffee trees, and all his children, except the little ones, help with the work.

Many families live on the *fazenda*, and most of them have four to six children. Their small houses are built of bricks and plaster, and roofed with tiles. The bricks are made in the brickyard on the *fazenda*.

*When Lúcia works, she wears
a big straw hat and a scarf under it
to keep the dust from her hair.*

Lúcia's father, Senhor Ferreira, was named João Batista after John-the-Baptist. In 1880, before João Batista was born, his family came to Brazil from Portugal. There, and in Brazil, too, it is the custom to name children after saints.

When João Batista was young, there was no school on the *fazenda*. So he never learned to read or write his native language, Portuguese. But now his children go to school and learn to read and write before they are old enough to start working in the coffee fields.

Senhor Ferreira wears a straw hat, too, for protection against the sun.

*Fausto is
ready for work
in the coffee fields.
He works with
a long rake.*

Lúcia has two brothers—Celso, aged seventeen, and Fausto, aged eleven, who also work with their father. And she has three little sisters who stay at home with their mother, Dona Ernestina. The little girls play in the yard around the house. The family cannot afford real toys, but the children have a good time playing with empty cans and kitchen utensils. The old hunting dog, Certeza, stays with them. He is lean and often hungry, for in a large family there is not much food left over for a dog!

The Fazenda Santa Bárbara covers many acres and belongs to a rich and distinguished man, Dr. Mário Carvalho da Rocha. He lives in the great city of São Paulo, about 160 miles to the east, and depends on an overseer to manage the *fazenda* for him. But he visits the *fazenda* at least once a month. He always brings his family to stay for the summer months, from December to March.

The Carvalho family fly from São Paulo in their own airplane. Their big house stands on a hill and has fine gardens around it and a swimming pool. The house is often filled with guests.

Like little girls everywhere, Lúcia's sisters play in the yard with kitchen things for toys.

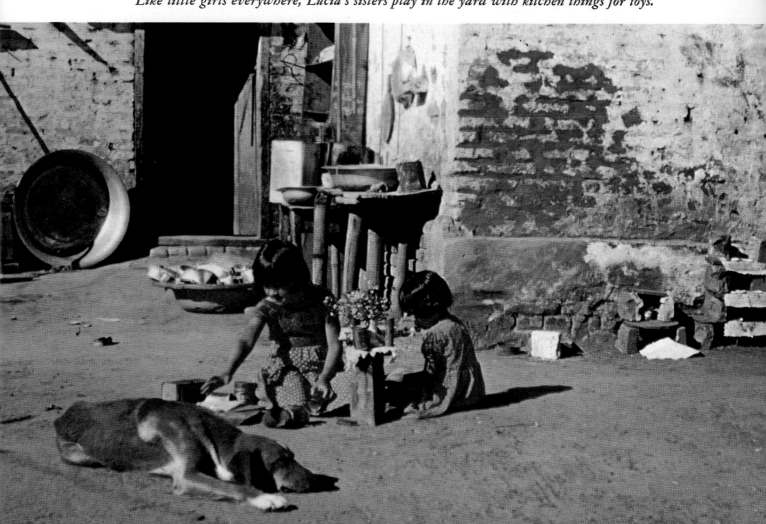

Dona Ernestina's gold earrings were brought by her grandmother from Portugal. She wears them always.

One cool morning Lúcia got up as usual long before dawn. She heard her mother making a fire in the wood stove to cook breakfast. Dona Ernestina prepared strong, black coffee and a *virado de feijão* —a dish of leftover boiled beans recooked with corn meal, lard, and onions.

After drinking her last cup of hot, sweet coffee, Lúcia went to the bedroom to put on a pair of long trousers underneath her dress. These would protect her legs from flies and from scratches as she worked among the coffee trees. Her father urged her to hurry. It was a long walk from their house to the grove where they would work, and the Ferreiras must not be late. Lúcia followed her father and brothers outside.

Dona Ernestina waved goodbye as the workers set off in the early morning.

At home Dona Ernestina was busy. She scoured her pots and pans with fine sand until they shone. Then she took some clothes to the creek to wash them. She rubbed them with soap she had made herself and beat them against a board to loosen the red dust. Then she spread the clothes on low bushes to dry.

The trees in the coffee fields are planted in long, straight rows, with spaces between them. The spaces are wide enough to allow Dr. Mário's little jeep to pass along. Dr. Mário is proud of his *fazenda*. Every time he comes, he spends many hours driving all over it with his overseer.

Coffee seedlings need much care. The ground around them must be weeded regularly and they must

Dr. Mário drove in his jeep between the rows of coffee trees, which stretched far into the distance.

Dr. Mário and the overseer watched the workers harvesting the coffee berries.

be well protected. Often little fences are built around the young plants to keep too much sun or wind from them. And small dikes are made to keep heavy rains from washing away the soil and the seedlings with it.

Sometimes on winter nights—often in August —frost harms the trees and may even kill some. The loss is great, for young coffee trees take five to six years to grow before they produce much.

Today Dr. Mário arrived early. He left the jeep from time to time to watch the workers. It was harvest time, and everyone was busy picking the coffee berries, sifting them, and putting them into sacks. Each worker had his own job to do.

Senhor Ferreira stripped the branches of the coffee trees.

Lúcia's father and her brother Celso could reach the upper branches of the coffee trees. So it was their job to strip the berries from the high branches. This each did by holding the end of a branch in one hand and pulling off all the berries, leaves, and twigs with one movement of the other hand. The work was easy but hard on the hands!

The berries they picked fell to the ground with the leaves and twigs. Then Fausto made them into neat piles with his wooden rake.

Lúcia separated the berries from the leaves and twigs. To do this she used a big wire sieve. She filled her sieve from a pile of berries, leaves, and twigs, and tossed them high in the air with a twirling motion.

Since the berries were heavier than the leaves and twigs, they fell back quickly into the sieve while the leaves and twigs were still in the air. Before the leaves and twigs could fall into the sieve, Lúcia moved it quickly aside to let them drop to the ground.

As Lúcia worked, dust flew in the air and made her sneeze. Fausto laughed and called out, *"Deus te abençoe!"* (God bless you!). And Lúcia replied, *"Obrigadinha!"* (Thanks very much!).

Lúcia and Fausto worked alongside their father, each doing a special job.

*Leaves and twigs flew in the air as Lúcia separated them
from the berries. Then she put the berries into a sack.*

Lúcia soon separated many pounds of coffee berries. She emptied each sieveful of berries into a large sack. During the day she filled many sacks with berries.

On his tour of the *fazenda*, Dr. Mário stopped to watch Lúcia at work. He praised her skill at tossing the berries and said she was an expert.

Suddenly he looked at his watch. It was nearly lunch time, and he called to the overseer to drive him back to the big house. The jeep roared off in a cloud of red dust, which sparkled in the air for several minutes before it slowly settled on the trees.

As Lúcia stood watching the jeep, she saw her mother and little sisters coming toward her. They were bringing lunch for the Ferreiras.

ona Ernestina carried four lunch pails. She had walked a long way in the hot sun. The little girls ran ahead of her and when they saw their father, they threw their arms around him. Lúcia put down her sieve and hurried to take the pails from her mother.

The lunch pails shone like silver. They were covered tightly to keep the food hot. Inside each was a mixture of black beans and rice. The workers were hungry. They sat down to eat in an open space between the coffee trees. Old Certeza lay in the shade of a tree. There would be no leftovers for him!

Dona Ernestina and the little girls brought pails of hot lunch for the workers.

Lúcia was hungry
and soon finished
some black beans and rice.

Dona Ernestina also brought bottles of hot coffee. Celso drank most of his at once. The others laughed because Brazilians never drink coffee until they have finished eating. But Celso liked coffee so much that he could not wait until he had finished his meal.

It was hot in the mid-day sun. But Lúcia was well shaded by her big straw hat as she rested.

After lunch the Ferreiras rested and talked.

Sacks of coffee berries were loaded on to wagons drawn by mule teams.

All that day about five hundred people worked in the coffee fields on the Fazenda Santa Bárbara. They did just what Lúcia and her father and brothers did—stripped the berries off the branches, raked them into piles, and put them into sacks.

As the hours passed, dozens of sacks were filled with berries and lay on the ground ready to be taken away on wagons.

The loaded wagons rolled along smoothly on rubber tires.

Late in the afternoon the wagons came. Each was drawn by six mules. A strong team was needed to pull a wagon loaded with heavy sacks of berries.

The men carried the sacks, one at a time, and piled them on the wagons. When each wagon was loaded, it moved off to the *terreiro*—the drying ground. All around were sounds of the jingling harness and of the drivers' voices as they urged their teams along.

When they reached the *terreiro*, the drivers lined up their wagons one behind the other ready for unloading. Then, standing on top of the pile of sacks, each driver lowered the sacks one by one on to the heads of men waiting below, who dumped them on the *terreiro*. Before long the *terreiro* looked like a checkerboard, with fat sacks lying in a regular pattern all over it.

The *terreiro* is vast—"big enough for a football field," as Celso once said. Each year at least 5000 sacks of berries are brought to the *terreiro* to be dried after the harvest. This is the time Dr. Mário likes best, for then he can see how large a crop Santa Bárbara will yield. But to Lúcia the best time is when the coffee trees bloom. Then she walks among the trees admiring the delicate blossoms and breathing their orange-scented perfume.

The sacks were unloaded one by one from the wagons and dumped on the terreiro.

When all the wagons were unloaded, the men untied the sacks and emptied them. The coffee berries spilled on to the ground and soon the *terreiro* was covered with them.

Then the men took long wooden rakes and spread out the mounds of berries until they were only two or three inches high. The warmth from the sun and from the brick floor of the *terreiro* began to dry the berries. The men raked over the berries so that they would dry evenly.

The overseer directed the men as they emptied the sacks of berries.

The men spread the berries over the ground with long rakes.

In the evening the men brought out sheets of canvas and covered the berries. The sky was cloudy and the overseer called to the men to hurry. The canvas would keep the coffee dry in case of rain. It would also protect the berries from the heavy dew of early morning.

The berries must be kept dry at this stage. The crop could be quickly damaged by dampness and the quality of the coffee spoiled. This would bring its price down and would mean a great loss for Dr. Mário.

Mules pulling wide rakes helped to spread the berries.

It took several days for the coffee berries to dry. Each day the men raked them over by hand or with the help of mules. The mules could pull much bigger rakes than the men could handle.

When the berries were thoroughly dry, the men put them back into the sacks and reloaded the sacks on to the wagons. The mule teams were brought out again and they pulled the wagons to a mill in the nearby town of Rio Bonito.

The mill is the central depot where berries from many *fazendas* are collected. Here the hulls of the berries are removed and the two little beans from each berry are cleaned, skinned, polished, and graded by size.

Most of the work at the mill is done by machines. There are even ovens in the mill where the berries can be dried much more quickly than in the sun. But some *fazenda* owners, like Dr. Mário, still use their own *terreiros* for drying berries.

When the beans have been graded, they are sent to the port of Santos, far away on the coast. From there they are shipped all over the world.

Finally, before the beans are shipped, samples of coffee are made from them. These samples are put into many separate cups for the coffee "taster."

At the port of Santos the coffee "taster" tests many samples of coffee.

He spends all day tasting coffee to test its quality. But he never swallows any; he spits out every mouthful into a large metal can. This tasting is done to ensure that all the coffee shipped from Brazil will be of high quality.

Much of the coffee grown in Brazil is shipped to the United States. Americans drink more coffee than any other people in the world and they consume a large amount of Brazil's immense crop.

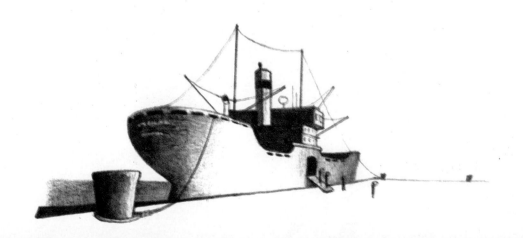

The Ferreira family do not spend all their time at work. On holidays and weekends Senhor Ferreira and the boys often go fishing, or hunting in the nearby forest. Some of their neighbors go hunting with them and take their own dogs. But Certeza is always the leader of the pack. His name means "certainty," and he lives up to it, for he is a good hunter and often finds a deer. He is a favorite in the family, especially when he helps to provide venison for a stew. He is thin, but Senhor Ferreira assures the children that Certeza hunts better if he is a bit hungry!

"Certeza's a good hunter," said Senhor Ferreira. "We'll have partridge for Sunday dinner!"

Fausto and his father watched the storekeeper write down the amount of their purchases.

On Saturday Fausto went with his father to the general store on the *fazenda*. They bought rice, beans, flour, and salt; and also kerosene, matches, and light bulbs. The storekeeper weighed each item of food on his scales. Then he wrote in his account book the quantity and the price beside Senhor Ferreira's name. Fausto handed his father an old, clean pillowcase they had brought with them for a shopping bag, and the storekeeper put their things inside it.

The store on the *fazenda* belongs to Dr. Mário, and shopping at the store is done only by the men. Most of the men shop there for their families because it is near their homes and because they can buy things on credit. The total amount due for their purchases is deducted from their wages at the end of each month. Sometimes the father of a large family, like Senhor Ferreira, cannot meet one bill before the next one is started, and then he is in debt!

When Senhor Ferreira and Fausto returned home, Dona Ernestina was making coffee. She used beans toasted almost black and ground to a fine powder. First, she boiled water on the wood stove. Then she added about ten big spoonfuls of coffee and stirred vigorously to prevent the foaming coffee from boiling over. After a few minutes, she poured the coffee into a linen bag hanging from a wooden frame. The coffee dripped through the bag into a coffee pot below. When all the coffee had dripped through, she put the pot at the back of the stove to keep the coffee hot until after the evening meal.

Every evening Dona Ernestina prepares a hot dinner for her family. She cooks rice and beans. With this she serves bread and sometimes a salad. The family eat at the big kitchen table.

The next day was Sunday—a special day for the Ferreira family. They all took baths in a big tub and then put on clean clothes. After breakfast Lúcia and Fausto went outside to play *peteca*, a game like shuttlecock played with the palm of the hand instead of a racket. But Fausto preferred *bocce*, a kind of bowling introduced by immigrants from Italy many years ago. So he went off to join his friends in a quick game before church time.

Celso and some older boys played *futebol*, or soccer—the most popular game in Brazil.

Lúcia's peteca *is made of leather and long feathers.*

Fausto took his turn at bocce *while his friends looked on.*

By eight o'clock in the morning Dona Ernestina had dressed the little girls and called the boys from their games. Everyone was ready to go to Mass. With other families from the *fazenda*, the Ferreiras walked several miles to church in Rio Bonito. They walked along the brick sidewalks of the town and past many fine houses.

Rio Bonito was once a village, but it grew rapidly when it became a center for processing coffee.

Wearing their Sunday clothes, the Ferreiras walked to church in Rio Bonito.

The tower of the church has a tiled dome, which reminds Lúcia of an upside-down pineapple.

The church is big and impressive. But it cannot hold all the people who come from miles around to attend Mass every Sunday. Many have to stand at the back of the church, and some even hear Mass outside on the steps.

After Mass the Ferreiras went to the market stands set up by farmers under the trees. Many kinds of fruit and vegetables were on sale. Dona Ernestina bought some lettuce, onions, and a cucumber to make a salad for Sunday dinner.

That day Lúcia's friend Cecília came to dinner. She lived with her family just down the road. Dona Ernestina had prepared a special treat—young partridge meat with brown gravy. Her husband and the boys and Certeza had had good luck hunting!

After the meat, Dona Ernestina served Lúcia's favorite pudding. This was made of fine rice flour,

Cabbages and other vegetables were on sale in the outdoor market.

Dona Ernestina served dinner to her family and Lúcia's friend Cecília.

cooked with vanilla to sweeten it, and served with apricot preserve. Cecília said it was delicious!

As usual, Celso finished his meal quickly and asked for coffee. "The best part of dinner is the coffee," he said.

They all laughed when Celso looked into his cup and said, "I recognize this coffee. It's made from beans I picked!"